· ZEN ·
WISDOM

*Daily Teachings
from the
Zen Masters*

TIMOTHY FREKE

Sterling Publishing Co., Inc.
New York

Library of Congress
Cataloging-in-Publication Data Available

1 2 3 4 5 6 7 8 9 10

Published in 1997 by Sterling Publishing Company, Inc
387 Park Avenue South, New York, N.Y. 10016

Originally published in Great Britain in 1997 by Godsfield Press
Laurel House, Station Approach, New Alresford, Hampshire SO24 9JH, U.K.

Copyright © 1997 Godsfield Press

Text © 1997 Timothy Freke

Designed and produced by
THE BRIDGEWATER BOOK COMPANY LTD

Picture research by Vanessa Fletcher

Distributed in Canada by Sterling Publishing
c/o Canadian Manda Group, One Atlantic Avenue, Suite 105
Toronto, Ontario, Canada M6K 3E7

Printed and bound in Singapore

ISBN 0-8069-9977-2

Acknowledgments are gratefully made to the following publishers for permission to use material in this publication.

HUMPHREYS, CHRISTMAS *Teach Yourself Zen* Hodder and Stoughton, 1962
SUZUKI, D.T. *An Introduction to Zen Buddhism* Rider, 1969
SUZUKI, SHUNRYU *Zen Mind, Beginner's Mind* Weatherhill, 1970
THIEN-AN, THICH *Zen Philosophy, Zen Practice,* Dharma Publishing, 1975
WATTS, ALAN *The Spirit of Zen* Grove Press, 1958

THIS BOOK IS DEDICATED
TO NOTHING
AND ALL THE NO ONES
THAT IT CONTAINS

C O N T E N T S

INTRODUCTION

In the sixth century a wandering Indian sage named Bodhidharma came to China. He was the latest in a long line of enlightened masters that originated with the Buddha himself and was honored as the 28th Patriarch of Buddhism. His teachings were uncompromisingly direct and experiential, aiming to transmit the essence of Buddhism without recourse to dogmas or superstition. His legacy was a vibrant and colorful approach to Buddhism called "Buddhahridaya," "The Doctrine of the Buddha-heart," which claims Bodhidharma as its founder and first Patriarch. In China this school became more commonly known as Ch'an, from the Sanskrit word "Dhyana" meaning meditation. In the 12th century, when it reached Japan, it acquired the familiar name of Zen.

On his arrival in China, Bodhidharma at first found no students capable of receiving his direct transmission of enlightenment, so he is said to have quietly meditated for nine years facing a wall. Meditation is the central practice of Zen Buddhism, through which students may enter into an exploration of consciousness and see deeply into their true nature. But meditation is not Zen, it is only a tool on a journey toward a realization that transcends all practices and philosophy. This experience is a direct encounter with the Truth. It is the realization of the essential Oneness of all things; that the apparent separateness experienced between one's self and the rest of the world is an illusion caused by differentiating everything into this and that, good and bad, desired and undesired.

When the mind is still, the student of Zen experiences that there is no separate self that was born and will die, but only consciousness itself, within which everything has its existence. Everything, including one's own self, is experienced as a transitory form, empty of independent reality. Everything is subsumed within an all-embracing love that unites existence into one mysterious whole. Such statements as these, however, are only philosophy. The Zen experience is not an idea to be grasped by the mind. It is more like having the clearest, most inspiring thought you can possibly imagine – except without the thought!

Although enlightenment may sound strange and otherworldly, it is actually the immediate perception of the obvious. It is found here and now in the daily unfolding of the ordinary lives we are already living. The Truth, we are told again and again, is staring us in the face. Zen is just being with what is, without judgments or opinions. Zen is you reading these words. Zen is life – completely natural and without any artificiality. It is something so intimate and apparent that it defies language and so can never be satisfactorily captured by words.

The Zen masters often appear to contradict themselves because they know that anything they say must necessarily be ultimately untrue and misleading, and so having said one thing they may equally well say the opposite. This is why they resort to the seemingly absurd and illogical to break us out of the prison of conceptual thought into a direct appreciation of life as it is. The masters compare their teachings to a finger pointing at the moon. The finger is not the moon, and to see the moon for oneself one's attention must follow where the finger points and not remain attached to the pointing finger. Zen teachings and practices, reverence for the Buddha, respect for Zen masters, study of the scriptures, even the desire for illumination – all are potential distractions from the spontaneous realization of enlightenment. For Zen to have performed its function it must self-destruct to leave the student free to enjoy a natural state of being, the realization of which is its only purpose.

BURN THIS BOOK

I have always associated book burning with Nazi tyranny and small-minded censorship; but I must confess to having burned one book myself, not, however, because I found it appalling or perverse, but rather because its message reached me so clearly. At the time I was in a long period of retreat in a little cottage in the country, sitting by the fire on a winter's evening reading *The Way of Zen* by Alan Watts. The more I read, the more the irony of my predicament became evident to me. I had come to spend some intensive time exploring consciousness and found the wisdom of the Zen masters insightful and relevant, yet with one voice they were asserting that the enlightenment experience could not be conveyed by words, but only found for oneself by looking within. In a sudden rush of realization I spontaneously threw the little book into the flames and calmly walked upstairs to my meditation room to investigate the matter first hand. The book had done its job admirably. It had self-destructed and faced me back toward myself.

Now, I am not suggesting that you literally burn this book. Books can be a constant source of the inspiration needed by spiritual adventurers, and this one in particular has been specifically designed to give a daily dose of insight from some of the greatest explorers of consciousness that the world has seen. While words cannot contain the Truth, they may help burn up the illusions that obscure us from our own natural state of enlightenment, and in so doing become a redundant pile of ashes themselves. These quotes and stories are offered, then, as objects of contemplation that may act as mind-bombs to explode the experience of separateness within which we are imprisoned – setting us free to delight in the wonderful miracle of life as it is.

THE TEN BULLS

Although enlightenment is a spontaneous and immediate awakening, such a profound shift in consciousness may take years of spiritual maturation. Some schools of Zen have emphasized the gradual nature of awakening, while others have used techniques to facilitate a sudden breakthrough into realization. From the Zen understanding, however, there is no contradiction here. Water may boil suddenly, but it heats gradually. A student may experience a spontaneous enlightenment, but only when his or her life has prepared the student for such an eventuality. Although enlightenment comes of itself, unenlightened human consciousness is time-bound and experiences a development toward this final freedom from the illusion of separateness.

The traditional Zen story of "The Ten Bulls," based on a much older Taoist tale, is a remarkable spiritual allegory of the stages of gradual awakening that a student of Zen will experience. This yearbook is divided into sections corresponding to these steps to enlightenment, each beginning with a pertinent verse and comments written by the 12th–century Chinese master Kuo-an Shih-yuan, which are followed by appropriate thoughts for each day. The Zen journey is not linear, however, and the whole Truth is there from the beginning and present throughout. This story is not a definitive template of a necessary development, and many seekers find themselves at different stages at different times. It is, nevertheless, an insightful metaphor, in which the bull represents the seeker's self, that he must find, master, and eventually relinquish altogether.

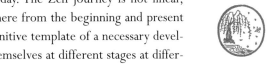

SEARCHING FOR THE BULL

The journey begins as an exhausting search for an elusive quarry. The seeker is pictured in search of himself, but all he can find is rustling leaves and singing cicadas, and he does not yet realize that these are the very clues he seeks. During this stage the student is often confused and discouraged. He doesn't really even know what it is he is looking for. Zen sounds strange and obscure, yet something in it inexplicably attracts him, nevertheless. Kuo-an Shih-yuan writes:

> In search of the bull,
> I fight my way through forests,
> following the course of unnamed rivers,
> lost on meandering mountain paths.
> Exhausted and despairing,
> I can find nothing but rustling leaves,
> and the singing of cicadas at nightfall.

Why search for a bull that has never been lost? The bull only appears lost because the oxherd is lost in the experience of separateness. His home becomes ever more distant. He reaches many crossroads in life, but does not know which road to follow. Desire and fear burn in him like a fire, and ideas of right and wrong imprison him.

1

JANUARY

Student: *"What is Zen?"*

Nan-ch'uan: *"Ordinary mind is very Zen."*

Student: *"Should we try to get it?"*

Nan-ch'uan: *"As soon as you try you miss it."*

2

JANUARY

We are like someone immersed in water,
who complains of nothing to drink.

HSUEH-FENG

3

JANUARY

Wise listeners, the wisdom of enlightenment
is inherent in each of us. We fail to recognize
it because of delusion of mind, and so to know
our own essence of Mind we seek the teachings
of the enlightened.

HUI-NENG

4

JANUARY

Student: *"What is the path to liberation?"*

Seng-t'san: *"Who binds you?"*

Student: *"No one binds me?"*

Seng-t'san: *"Why then do you want to be liberated?"*

5

JANUARY

There are in Zen no sacred books of dogmatic tenets.
If I am asked, therefore, what Zen teaches, I would answer
Zen teaches nothing. Whatever teachings there are in Zen,
they come out of one's own mind. We teach ourselves;
Zen merely points the way.

D.T. SUZUKI

6
JANUARY

Tsing-ping asked master T'sui-wei, "What is the fundamental principle of Buddhism?" "I will tell you later when there is no one else around," said the master. Later, when they were alone, Tsing-ping again asked his question. The master led his student out into the bamboo grove, but he still said nothing. Tsing-ping pressed him for an answer. T'sui-wei whispered, "Look how high these bamboos are! And how short those over there!"

7
JANUARY

The student asked the master, "What is the deepest meaning of Buddhism?" The master bowed deeply to his pupil.

8
JANUARY

If you meet a wise man and you do not say anything to him nor keep silence, how would you question him?

FA-YEN

9
JANUARY

A Buddhist philosopher named Tao-kwang asked a Zen master, "When attempting to educate oneself in the nature of Truth, what frame of mind should be adopted?" The master replied, "There is no mind to be framed, nor is there any Truth to be educated in." The philosopher responded, "If what you say is true, why do monks gather around you to be educated in Truth?" The master answered, "I have no space – how could monks gather around me? I have no tongue – so how could I teach others?" The philosopher exclaimed, "That is a shameless lie!" "I have already told you I have no tongue," responded the master, "so it is impossible for me to lie." Despairingly the philosopher said, "I simply do not understand your logic." "I don't understand myself," concluded the master.

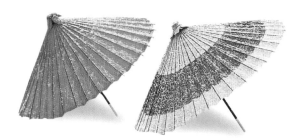

10

JANUARY

While striving to catch the butterfly of Zen in the net of reason we must know that the task is hopeless.

CHRISTMAS HUMPHREYS

11

JANUARY

The aim of Zen is to focus the attention on reality itself, instead of on our intellectual and emotional reactions to reality – reality being the ever-changing, ever-growing, indefinable something known as "life," which will never stop for a moment for us to fit it satisfactorily into any rigid system of pigeon-holes and ideas.

ALAN WATTS

12

JANUARY

Wishing to entice the blind,
The Buddha playfully let words escape
from his golden mouth;
Heaven and earth are filled, ever since,
with entangling briars.

DAI-O KOKUSHI

13

JANUARY

Zen claims to be Buddhism, but all the Buddhist teachings as propounded in the sutras and sastras are treated by Zen as mere waste paper whose utility consists in wiping off the dirt of intellect and nothing more.

D.T. SUZUKI

15

JANUARY

Master Ikkyu advised that before intellectual study of Buddhist texts, and endless chanting of the sutras, a student of Zen should learn how to read the love letters sent by the snow, the wind, and the rain.

16

JANUARY

Student: *"Who preaches the wisdom of the Buddha?"*
Nanyang: *"Walls and stones."*
Student: *"How can they teach anything –*
they are insentient?"
Nanyang: *"They are always eloquently teaching the truth."*
Student: *"I can't hear it."*
Nanyang: *"But that doesn't mean everyone can't."*
Student: *"Who hears it then?"*
Nanyang: *"All the sages do."*

17

JANUARY

Do not search for truth.
Just stop having opinions.

SENG-T'SAN

14

JANUARY

While staying at a shrine, master Tan-hsia was feeling cold, so he took a wooden statue of the Buddha off the altar and threw it into the fire. The keeper of the shrine was dismayed and angry. In response, the master began looking among the ashes. "What are you doing?" inquired the keeper of the Shrine. "Looking for holy relics in the ashes," replied the master. "You won't find them in the ashes of a wooden statue," said the Keeper. "If that is so," the master concluded, "can I have another couple of Buddhas for the fire to keep me warm?"

18
JANUARY

The master rose to give his sermon, but simply stretched out his arms and remained silent. He was about to leave the hall when a student asked why he had said nothing. The master replied, "The scriptures are expounded by the scripture teachers and the commentaries by the commentators. Why do you wonder at me? Am I not a Zen Master?"

20
JANUARY

Student: *"How can I find my Buddha-nature?"*
Master: *"You have no Buddha-nature."*
Student: *"What about animals?"*
Master: *"They do have Buddha-nature."*
Student: *"Then why do I not have Buddha-nature?"*
Master: *"Because you have to ask."*

19
JANUARY

"All this Zen stuff is nonsense," said the skeptic. "You are perfectly correct," responded the master, "but this is a teaching I normally reserve for only my most advanced students."

21
JANUARY

A renowned professor once visited master Nan-in to learn about Zen. The master politely poured him some tea, but didn't stop pouring and the cup overflowed all over his guest. The professor shouted in distress for him to stop. The master replied, "The cup is full of tea and can contain no more unless I first empty it. In the same way your mind is full of ideas and there is no room for my teachings, unless you empty it."

JANUARY

Master Hui-hai was asked, "Are Taoism, Confucianism, and Buddhism three different doctrines or the same?" He replied, "To those with great understanding they are the same. To those of average understanding they are different. They all come from the one Truth, but an analytical approach makes them seem three. However, whether someone achieves enlightenment or remains deluded depends on the seeker, not on differences in doctrine."

JANUARY

When master Mu-nan made Shoju his successor he gave him an old book, saying, "This book of wisdom has been written in by generations of masters. I myself have added my own comments and understanding. Now it is yours." Shoju was disinterested. "I learned Zen from you without words," he said. "I have no use for this book – you keep it." "It belongs to you," said Mu-nan, "as a symbol of the teachings you have received – here." Shoju took the book and immediately threw it into the fire they were both warming themselves around. Mu-nan, who never got angry, yelled, "What are you doing?" Shoju responded calmly, "What are you saying?"

JANUARY

Don't you realize that if you simply have no concepts and no anxiety, you'll see the Buddha standing before you.

HUANG-PO

JANUARY

There is in Zen nothing to explain, nothing to teach,
that will add to your knowledge. Unless it grows out
of yourself no knowledge is really yours, it is only a
borrowed plumage.

D.T. SUZUKI

26

JANUARY

T'ao-ch'ein asked a fellow monk to accompany him on a long journey to help him in his study of Zen. His friend said, "I'll certainly try to help you in any way I can, but there are some things you must do yourself." "What do you mean?" asked T'ao-ch'ein. His friend replied, "Well, my eating or drinking will not fill your stomach. When you want to urinate, there's nothing I can do about it. And only you can make your body walk along the road." This answer opened T'ao-chien's mind and he made the journey alone.

27

JANUARY

I was born alone
I will die alone.
And between these two
I am alone day and night.

SENGAI

28

JANUARY

If you do not get it from yourself,
where will you go for it?

ZEN SAYING

29

JANUARY

Student: *"Is there anything more miraculous
than the wonders of nature?"*
Master: *"Yes. Your appreciation of these wonders."*

30

JANUARY

Student: *"All these natural wonders – the trees,
mountains, and earth – where do they come from?"*
Master: *"Where does your question come from?"*

31

JANUARY

Student: *"How can I perceive my Self-nature?"*
Master: *"That which perceives is your Self-nature.
Without it there could be no perception."*

FEBRUARY

Before enlightenment, Buddhas are no different than ordinary people. After enlightenment, ordinary people at once become Buddhas.

HUI-NENG

FEBRUARY

When an ignorant person understands –
he becomes a saint.
But when a saint understands –
he becomes an ignorant person.

EKAI

FEBRUARY

Delusion and the Awakening –
both can come or go slowly or suddenly.

SHEN-HUI

4

FEBRUARY

This glimpse of the Absolute is to be sought here and now, not only in the mystical sense of Here and Now, because there is nought else, but literally in doing what we are doing now, be it meditation, earning a living, or washing-up.

CHRISTMAS HUMPHREYS

5

FEBRUARY

Zen reveals itself in the most uninteresting and uneventful life of a plain man in the street, recognizing the fact of living in the midst of life as it is lived.

D.T. SUZUKI

6

FEBRUARY

The ways to the One are as many as the lives of men.

ZEN SAYING

7

FEBRUARY

It is a rare privilege to be born human, as we happen to be. If we do not achieve enlightenment in this life. When do we expect to achieve it?

ECHU

8

FEBRUARY

Birth and death is a grave event;
How transient is life!
Every minute is to be grasped.
Time waits for nobody.

INSCRIPTION ON A ZEN GONG

9

FEBRUARY

Zen is life; to chase after Zen is like chasing one's own shadow, and all the time one is running away from the sun.

ALAN WATTS

FINDING THE FOOTPRINTS

Through contemplating the Buddha's teachings of the essential Oneness of all things, the seeker starts to discover that the bull's footprints are obvious everywhere. He has not yet found the bull, but he has discovered tracks. He has not yet achieved the Zen vision, but he has perceived the path. He has realized that, in the words of the Buddha, "with our thoughts we create the world." At this stage a student starts to feel enthusiastic and optimistic, as if enlightenment is just around the next corner. Kuo-an Shih-yuan writes:

> *Footprints —*
> *under trees by the riverbank,*
> *amongst the fragrant grasses,*
> *in the remote mountains.*
> *These tracks are as omnipresent as the sky*
> *and as obvious as my own nose.*

Through the guidance of the Buddha's wisdom the oxherd has come to understand something – he has found footprints. He has realized that just as many objects are made from one metal, so all things in the objective world are reflections of the self. However, he cannot discriminate between truth and falsehood. He has found the path but not yet entered the gate.

10
FEBRUARY

The great Indian sage Bodhidharma was the 28th Buddhist Patriarch. In the sixth century he visited China and became the first Patriarch of Zen. Buddhism was already well established in China as a religion, but they had never had an enlightened master, so the Buddhist Emperor Wu was very eager to meet Bodhidharma. He invited the sage to his palace and asked him, "I have built many monasteries, performed countless good deeds, and been a generous patron of Buddhism. What merit have I earned?" Bodhidharma replied, "None whatsoever."

11
FEBRUARY

The astonished Emperor Wu asked Bodhidharma, "What is the holy truth of Buddhism?" Bodhidharma replied, "Limitless emptiness – and nothing holy in it."

12
FEBRUARY

The confused and somewhat angry Emperor Wu demanded, "If you say all is nothing, then tell me who are you?" Bodhidharma replied, "I have no idea." The Emperor was completely at a loss, and Bodhidharma, seeing that there was no one ready to appreciate his teachings, took himself off and sat in meditation facing a wall for nine years.

13
FEBRUARY

A special transmission outside the scriptures;
No dependence upon words and letters;
Direct pointing to the heart of man;
Seeing into one's own nature.

THE MESSAGE OF BODHIDHARMA

14

FEBRUARY

This is the Great Mystery.
You do and do not exist.

SHEN T'SING

15

FEBRUARY

Our Buddha-nature is there from the very beginning.
It is like the sun emerging from behind clouds.
It is like a mirror which reflects perfectly when
it is wiped clean and returned to its original clarity.

HO-SHAN

16

FEBRUARY

However much you try through logical reasoning and
definition to know your original face before your birth or
your original home, you are doomed to failure.
Even if you search the core of your being, becoming full
of questioning, you won't find anything that you could call a
personal mind or essence. Yet when someone calls your
name, something in you hears and responds.
Find out who it is! Find out now!

BASSUI TOKUSHO

17

FEBRUARY

What was your original face
before your parents were born?

ZEN KOAN

18

FEBRUARY

Heroes become Buddhas with one thought,
but lazy people are given the three collections of scriptures
to work through.

ZEN SAYING

19

FEBRUARY

"**E**nlightenment" and "Nirvana"? They are dead trees
to fasten a donkey to. The scriptures? They are bits of paper
to wipe mud from your face. The four merits and ten steps?
They are ghosts in their graves. What can these things have
to do with you becoming free?

TE-SHAN

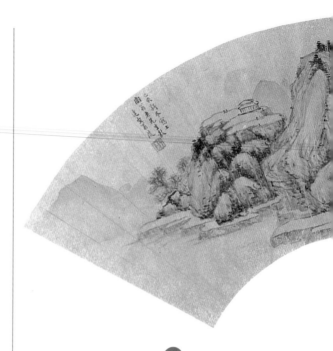

20

FEBRUARY

You fools! What are you running after so intently?
Why are you trying to put a head on top of your head?
Your head is already exactly where it needs to be.

LIN-CHI

21

FEBRUARY

When asked how he disciplined himself in Zen, a master
answered, "When I am hungry I eat, when I'm tired I sleep."
"But that is what everyone does," said his questioner.
"Not at all," replied the master. "When most people eat they
do not eat, but think of other things; when they sleep,
they do not sleep, but dream of all sorts of nonsense.
This is the difference."

22

FEBRUARY

When you boil rice,
know that the water is your own life.

ZEN SAYING

I have no secrets to teach you, and if I tried you may well make fun of me. Anyway, how could any understanding that I have become your understanding.

KUEI-SHAN

Zen abhors repetition or imitation of any kind, for it kills.

D.T. SUZUKI

It is right to spare the lives of all conscious beings, such as animals, and even insects. But what about killing time? And wasting wealth? There are many ways of killing. Preaching without being enlightened for example. This is killing Buddhism.

GA-SAN

23
FEBRUARY

Frequently the Zen masters referred to each other as "old rice bags" and with other uncomplimentary terms, not out of any professional jealousy, but because it amused them to think that they and their wise and venerated brothers were supposed by ordinary standards to be so especially holy, whereas they had all realized that everything was holy, even cooking pots and odd leaves blown about by the wind, and that there was nothing particularly venerable about themselves.

ALAN WATTS

When master Hui-neng was questioned about his training system he replied: "I would not be being straight with you if I claimed to have a system. I just do what I can to free my students from their own bondage, by any means their individual case may require."

 FEBRUARY

One day master Keichu's assistant presented him with a calling card from a guest which read "Kitagaki, Governor of Kyoto." "I don't want to see him," yelled the master, so the assistant returned the card to the distinguished visitor. The visitor, realizing his error, took a pencil and scribbled out the words, "Governor of Kyoto" and asked the assistant to represent his card to the master who said, "Oh it's Kitagaki – show him in."

 FEBRUARY

It is nonsense to insist that we cannot achieve enlightenment without learned and pious teachers. Because wisdom is innate, we can all enlighten ourselves.

HUI-NENG

1

MARCH

A student was caught stealing and his fellows asked master Bankei to expel him from the community. The master ignored the request, but the student stole again.

The others drew up a petition demanding his expulsion, stating that otherwise they would all leave. Bankei called them together and said, "You are wise, my friends. You know right from wrong. You can go somewhere else to study, but this poor fellow – who will teach him if I do not? I must keep him as my student even if the rest of you leave." The student who had stolen was overcome with tears and never stole again.

2

MARCH

The monks asked master Pai-chang to give a sermon. He replied that he would talk about Zen later, and that they should get on with their farming. After work had finished the master was requested to fulfill his promise, whereupon he opened both his arms as if to embrace the whole universe.

3

MARCH

A novice asked a master for instruction. The master replied, "Have you had your breakfast yet?" "I have," said the student. "Then wash your bowl," said the master.

4

MARCH

Those who are content to be nothing special are noble people. Don't strive. Be ordinary.

LIN-CHI

MARCH

A monk asked master Wei-shan why Bodhidharma
had come to China. In answer, the master held up
his teaching stick.

MARCH

M aster Hsiang-yen asked a monk, "Do you understand the
meaning of Wei-shan holding up his stick?"
The monk replied, "The master's idea was to point to
objective reality – to demonstrate the Truth beyond
concepts." "Your theories are alright, but limited,"
said Hsiang-yen. "What is your understand then?"
asked the student. Hsiang-yen held up his teaching stick.

7

MARCH

Our lives are based on what is reasonable and common sense; truth is apt to be neither.

CHRISTMAS HUMPHREYS

8

MARCH

Let go of your hold.

HAKUIN

9

MARCH

Spring flowers, autumn moon,
Summer breeze, winter snow —
When the mind is free from
unnecessary thoughts,
Every season is just perfect!

EKAI

10

MARCH

In a certain sense Zen is feeling life instead of feeling something about life.

ALAN WATTS

11

MARCH

Vimalakirti asked Manjusri what was the Buddha's doctrine of nonduality. Manjusri answered, "The doctrine is realized by one who sees beyond forms and who knows beyond argument. This is my understanding – what is yours?" In response to this question, Vimalakirti closed his lips and was silent.

MARCH

Do you want the Truth?
Then abandon words and silence,
and live your own Zen.

EKAI

MARCH

A student came to the monastery to seek the truth of
Buddhism. "Why have you come to a monastery?"
asked the master. "Why do neglect you own precious
treasure at home?" "What is my treasure?"
asked the student. "The one who asks the question is
the treasure," replied the master.

MARCH

The Buddhas are all his servants. Who is he?
When you see him you will feel as if you have met
your own father at the end of the road.
You won't need to ask anyone else
if you are right or wrong.

EKAI

15

MARCH

Just get rid of the false and you will
automatically realize the true.

HO-SHAN

16

MARCH

What is the ultimate teaching of Buddhism?
You won't understand it until you have it.

SHIH-T'OU

17

MARCH

Hakuin boldly calligraphed the character for the word
for "DEATH," and then added, "If anyone can see into the
depths of this word he is a true hero."

18

MARCH

Shall I compare this life to a lightning
flash or a drop of dew?
Before I have even spoken these words,
it has passed.

SENGAI

19

MARCH

The secret is within your self.

HUI-NENG

20

MARCH

Zen is a way of being happy.

T'AO-SHAN

SEEING 3
THE BULL

At this stage the student catches a glimpse of his own true nature. When the world and the self are known to be One, the bull is seen everywhere, beyond description and penetrating all things. He has caught the vision, but it is fleeting. Kuo-an Shih-yuan writes:

> *Birdsong from within the branches,*
> *warm sun and cool breeze,*
> *green willows by the riverbank.*
> *There is nowhere for the bull to hide.*
> *Who could paint such a huge head*
> *and such penetrating horns?*

The oxherd listens hard and finds the way. His senses become harmonious and he sees into the source of things. It is obvious in everything he does. This unity is like salt in water. When he is completely clear, he will discover that even the smallest thing is not apart from the self.

21

MARCH

Someone may be deluded for lifetimes,
but may attain Buddhahood in a moment.

HUI-NENG

22

MARCH

How then do we know? By the intuition.
This intuition is direct and immediate in experience.
By it we know, as immediately as a hand that picks
up a red-hot instrument knows pain.

CHRISTMAS HUMPHREYS

23

MARCH

We see it, yet it is not seen.
We hear it, yet it is not heard.
We talk about it, yet it is not talked about.
We know it and yet it is not known.
Tell me, how does this happen?

YUAN-WU

24

MARCH

You cannot tread the Path
before you have became that Path yourself.

ZEN SAYING

25
MARCH

I remember when a boy lying on my back in the grass, gazing into the summer blue above me, and wishing I could melt into it – become a part of it. Now I think that in those days I was really close to a great truth – touching it in fact without the faintest suspicion of its existence. I mean the truth that the wish to become is reasonable in direct ratio to its largeness – or in other words that the more you wish to be, the wiser you are; while the wish to have is apt to be foolish in proportion to its largeness. Cosmic Law permits us very few of the countless things that we wish to have, but will help us to become all that we can possibly wish to be.

LAFCADIO HEARN

26
MARCH

When Zen wants you to taste the sweetness of sugar
it puts the required article in your mouth and
no further words are said.

D.T. SUZUKI

27
MARCH

Student: *"Show me the way to enlightenment."*
Master: *"Do you hear that babbling brook?"*
Student: *"Yes."*
Master: *"Enter there."*

28
MARCH

A Samurai warrior approached master Hakuin and asked, "What is hell and heaven?" The master took one look at the Samurai and started insulting him saying, "You are such a scruffy looking warrior you would never understand anything." The Samurai became furious and pulled out his sword. "There!" said Hakuin. "This is hell."
The Samurai had a flash of illumination and was overcome with gratitude, humbly bowing before the master. Hakuin said, "There! This is heaven."

29

MARCH

For someone with a special gift or a certain sharpness of mind, a gesture or a word is all that is needed to impart an immediate perception of Truth.

CHIANG CHIH-CHI

30

MARCH

One day a master was just about to give a sermon when a bird started to sing. The master said nothing and everyone listened to the bird. When the song stopped, the master announced that the sermon had been preached and went on his way.

31

MARCH

Zen masters are totally identified with Nature.

D.T. SUZUKI

1

APRIL

Buddhism has no room for special effort.
Just be ordinary and nothing special.
Eat and drink, then move your bowels and pass water,
and when you're tired go to sleep.
Fools will find me ridiculous,
but the wise will understand.

LIN-CHI

Master Tao-sheng believed that everything had Buddha-nature, which was a heresy at the time and he was expelled from the Buddhist community. Tao-sheng, however, was content to preach to the rocks, who it is said nodded in agreement. Years later, master Ungan remarked that the rocks had been nodding long before anyone had bothered to speak to them.

4

APRIL

Nature is much more concerned with play
than with reaching goals.

ALAN WATTS

5

APRIL

In some religions the Holy Man is a figure of adoration and renown. But many of the greatest Zen masters of the past behaved and looked like tramps, and were regarded as mildly mad. Only the few, with an opened eye of Buddhi, saw the greatness within the utterly happy but apparently irresponsible life of the sage.

CHRISTMAS HUMPHREYS

2

APRIL

There was nothing sentimental about the masters who used to box their disciple's ears to bring them to their sense, and who experienced life "close to Nature" not only when she was warm and pleasant but when she was freezing, wet, and stormy. The sentimental "lover of Nature" only sees one side of her face; when it is wet he goes indoors and speaks of the delightful hissing of the rain on leaves. He does not let it trickle down his neck.

ALAN WATTS

6

APRIL

Waiting
in the cloakroom
of Reality
I am scared –
like a shy adolescent at a party –
to knock (maybe)
and go in.
I'd rather look at the coats:
– try and figure out
who's already
Inside.

PETE RAWLINGS

7

APRIL

When you can tell which man has an open inner eye,
I will admit that you really have had a personal interview
with the ancient sages.

YUAN-WU

8

APRIL

An enlightened being is his own light.
He can see in the dark.
He turns on the light only for his guests.
He uses ideas only to illuminate his visitors.

SHEN T'SING

9

APRIL

Someone who has seen into his self-nature,
sees it whenever questioned about it.

HUI-NENG

10

APRIL

What is Mind? It is the true nature of all sentient beings.
It existed before your parents were born and so before our
own birth. It exists now, eternally unchanging.
It is called "one's Face before one's parents were born."
It does not come into existence at birth and it does not
disappear at death. It is not male or female. It is not good
or bad. It can't be compared with anything.
This is why it is called "Buddha-nature."

BASSUI TOKUSHO

11

APRIL

It is not one, not two, not both, and not neither.
You can't get hold of it. Don't try. For while the part sees
the Whole, there is no Zen, for there are still two things,
the part and the Whole. Zen awareness must be an expan-
sion of consciousness beyond all knowledge of any kind and
beyond all process.

CHRISTMAS HUMPHREYS

12

APRIL

Babbling about "Buddha" and "Dharma"
is an offense to both. Why break the quiet by talking
about silence? Why fracture reality by giving it a name?

SHEN T'SING

13

APRIL

It is the sufferings and insecurities of our lives that,
although painful and distressing, teach us not to cling on
to the impermanent things of this world.
Not even the greatest master could teach us so well.
We should honor and respect them,
not shun their company.

T'AO-SHAN

APRIL

Investigate your mind and realize your Buddha-nature —
that which never rests nor moves, neither starts nor stops.
You will have wasted your lifetime if you don't.

HUI-NENG

APRIL

It is wisdom that is seeking for wisdom.

SHUNRYU SUZUKI

APRIL

Finding the universal in every particular,
whether coming or going, they remain unmoving.
Finding the silence which contains thoughts,
whatever they do they hear the Truth.

HAKUIN

APRIL

Where there is beauty, there is ugliness.
When something is right, something else is wrong.
Knowledge and ignorance depend on each other.
Delusion and enlightenment condition each other.
It has been like this since the beginning.
How could it be otherwise now?
Wanting to chuck out one and hold on to the other
makes for a ridiculous comedy.
You must still deal with everything ever-changing,
even when you say it's all wonderful.

RYOKAN

APRIL

To follow the Way, do not push away anything –
even sensual experiences and thoughts.
In fact, to completely accept them is enlightenment.

SENG-T'SAN

APRIL

Just see that Buddhism is not found in the world,
but do not yet conclude that there is nothing
worldly about Buddhism.

DOGEN

APRIL

If you have sentiments about Buddhist teaching,
it becomes a worldly thing.
If you have no sentiments about worldly things,
they become Buddhist teaching.

ZEN PROVERB

尋牛

21

APRIL

Become a master of every situation,
and you will always be in the right place.

LIN-CHI

22

APRIL

You ask me how to practice Zen on your sickbed.
I ask you who is it that is sick? Who is practicing Zen?
Who you are? Do you know? Your whole being is
Buddha-nature. You are the Great Way — beyond all forms.
Is there any sickness in it?

LETTER FROM BASSUI TOKUSHO

23

APRIL

During a funeral a monk knocked on the coffin
and asked, "Is he dead or alive?" His master replied,
"I won't say alive, I won't say dead."

24

APRIL

Just as the highest and the lowest notes
are equally inaudible, so, perhaps, is the greatest sense
and the greatest nonsense equally unintelligible.

ALAN WATTS

25

APRIL

The heavy intellectuals are still dissecting
Zen in the laboratory and solemnly reporting
that there is nothing in it. How nearly right they are!

CHRISTMAS HUMPHREYS

26

APRIL

"**N**othing but lies come out of my mouth,"
said the master. "There – see! I've just done it again."

27

APRIL

Whose mouth could possibly be big enough
to describe things as they are?

ALAN WATTS

28

APRIL

There is nothing real in my teachings.
If you understand that you will be rich enough
to really enjoy yourself!

LIN-CHI

29

APRIL

Your treasure house is within you.
It holds all you will ever need.

HUI-HAI

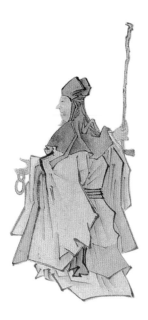

CAT**4**CHING
THE BULL

The seeker must now struggle to catch the bull. At this stage the student realizes that what he has found is not enlightenment, but a self that is uncontrollable and unruly, like a wild beast that he must master in order to progress further on his journey. He must overcome his own restless mind to sustain the Zen vision. Zen is experienced as a challenge to be faced, and the separate self as an obstacle to be overcome. The bull will not yield easily, however, finding refuge in inaccessible hiding places. In the same way the separate self of the student, when faced with disciplines like meditation, may cleverly find every excuse not to practice, or more subtle still, decide to reinvent itself with fantasies of being a special spiritual person. Kuo-an Shih-yuan writes:

> *I battle bravely to seize the bull —*
> *struggling with its ferocious will*
> *and inexhaustible strength,*
> *as it charges high into misty mountains*
> *and deep into inaccessible ravines.*

The bull that has been lost in the wilderness is found at last, but he is hard to control. He constantly longs for the sweet-smelling fields. His wild nature is unruly and does not wish to be tamed. If the oxherd wants the bull to be in complete harmony with himself, he will have to raise his whip.

APRIL

To realize Mind, begin by looking for the source of your thoughts. Whether asleep or working, standing or sitting, intensely ask yourself, "What is my mind?"

BASSUI TOKUSHO

MAY

One inch of meditation, one inch of Buddha;
So inch by inch, make the six-foot form of Buddha.

ZEN SAYING

MAY

When you are practicing zazen, do not try to stop your thinking. Let it stop by itself. If something comes into your mind, let it come in, and let it go out. It will not stay long. When you try to stop your thinking, it means you are bothered by it. Do not be bothered by anything. It appears as if something comes from outside your mind, but actually it is only the waves of your mind, and if you are not bothered by the waves, gradually they will become calmer and calmer. In five or at most ten minutes, your mind will be completely serene and calm.

SHUNRYU SUZUKI

MAY

Stop chasing after things. Let mildew form on your mouth. Have no resistance, like perfect silk. Only think of eternity. Be cold and lifeless as ashes from old incense in a deserted shrine.

SHIH-SHUANG

4
MAY

The person who dallies on the edge of the stream, wondering how best to take the plunge, testing the water with his toes, and thinking about how it will feel when he is in, soon gets into the habit of putting off the issue.
The Zen disciple must walk quietly to the edge and slip calmly into the water without further ado, without allowing himself time to conjure up fears and anxious speculations as to what it will be like, or to find elaborate reasons as to why he should not get in at once.

ALAN WATTS

5
MAY

From a well-worn path we step into fog wherein lies precipices, quagmires, and a howling wilderness. We must learn to walk on, through nonsense to a noble Non-sense, from the tram lines of a settled mind, through the trackless desert of no meaning, to the freedom of "a mind that alights nowhere," and is based forever on No-thought, No-purpose, and No-difference of any kind.

CHRISTMAS HUMPHREYS

6
MAY

A man asked, "How can one always be with Buddha?" The master replied, "Keep your mind still. Treat the outside world with serene acceptance. Remain absolutely empty and calm. This is the way to be with Buddha."

7
MAY

"Where are you going?" asked Tung-shan of a student who was sitting still with eyes shut. The student replied, "I am entering meditation." Tung-shan said, "Meditation has no gate. How can you enter into it?"

尋
牛

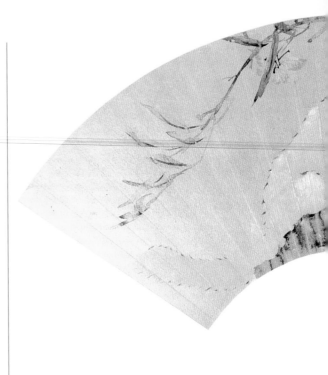

8

MAY

Four Zen pupils who were studying meditation had promised to observe a rule of silence for seven days. On the first day all were silent. Their meditation sessions had begun well, but when night came and the oil lamps were burning dimly, one of the pupils could not help himself exclaiming, "Someone should fix those lamps." The second pupil was shocked to hear him speak and cautioned him, "We are not supposed to say a word." "You idiots," said the third. "Now you've both spoken." "I am the only one who has not talked," proclaimed the fourth.

9

MAY

When you try to stop doing to achieve being, this very effort fills you with doing.

SENG-T'SAN

10

MAY

Student: *"I have nothing."*
Master: *"Then throw it away."*

11

MAY

Master Hogen asked a monk, "Look at this big old stone. Do you think it is inside or outside of your mind?" The monk replied, "According to Buddhist teachings, everything is a projection of the mind, so I conclude that it is inside my mind." Hogen commented, "Don't you get tired carrying around such a heavy stone?"

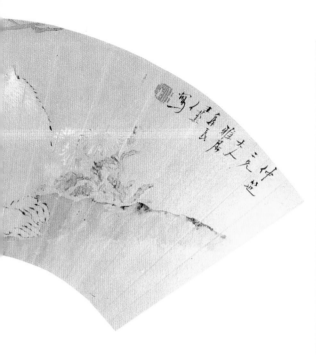

Student: *"The light of the Buddha's wisdom illuminates the whole world."*
Master: *"You are quoting scriptures aren't you?"*
Student: *"Yes."*
Master: *"You are lost. A greedy fish opens his mouth when he sees the hook."*

14
MAY

When one person tells a lie,
countless others tell it as a truth.

ZEN PROVERB

15
MAY

The Buddha is not the great goal
of those that follow the Way. Personally,
I see him as a privy hole and regard
the Bodhisattvas as jailers.

LIN-CHI

12
MAY

If your eyes are even slightly blurred,
all you see is hallucinations.

ZEN SAYING

16

MAY

There have never been any Buddhas, nor is there any holy teachings. Bodhidharma never came to the East, nor did he ever transmit any secret doctrine through the mind. Not understanding what this means, worldly people look for the truth outside of themselves. It is ironic that what they so desperately seek is under their own feet!

YUAN-WU

17

MAY

Look for Buddha outside your own mind, and Buddha becomes the devil.

DOGEN

18

MAY

The only way to Buddhahood is freeing your mind to be itself.

TAO-HSIN

19

MAY

If you want to achieve a certain thing you have to change into a certain person, but then you won't care about doing that certain thing.

DOGEN

20

MAY

Here it is – right now. Start thinking about it and you miss it.

HUANG-PO

21

MAY

Ikkyu visited a dying student and
asked if he required his help. The man replied,
"I don't need anything. I am just going to the changeless."
"If you think you are a something that can go anywhere,
you still need my teachings," replied Ikkyu.

22

MAY

onfused by thoughts,
we experience duality in life. Unencumbered by ideas,
the enlightened see the one Reality.

HUI-NENG

23

MAY

All life is changing, all the forms of it, and we flow with
the river or we refuse. If we happily flow we see, as science
sees, that things are really events in time and space, that
events are major and minor whirlpools on the river of time.
If we flow with the river, the ceaseless flow of our karma,
we can digest it, as it were, as we flow, and feel no suffering.
Accept it and we are one with it; resist it and we are hurt.

CHRISTMAS HUMPHREYS

24

MAY

e should find perfect existence through
imperfect existence.

SHUNRYU SUZUKI

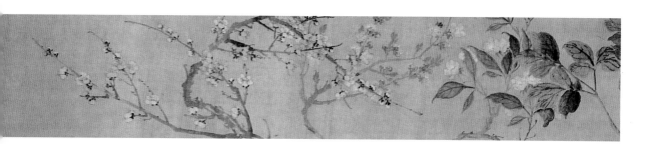

MAY

Look at that rainbow.
It is only when the sky cries
that you see the colors
in the light.

T'AO-SHAN

26

MAY

My detractors are actually good friends,
because if I am equanimous and accepting
the power of love and humility,
which is born of the Unborn,
grows within me.

YUNG-CHIA TA-SHIH

27

MAY

Master Seung Sahn taught that
"Zen mind is not Zen mind." He encouraged
his students to abandon narrow ideas
of Zen and hang on only to the question
"What is the best way of helping other people?"

28

MAY

Student: *"I am very discouraged.*
What should I do?"
Soen Nakagwa: *"Encourage others."*

29

MAY

Master Chu-hung was once writing a book
on the good deeds of Zen monks when a student asked him,
"What is the use of writing such a book when in Zen there
is nothing good or not good?"
The master slapped him on the face.
The furious monk was about to leave when the master
smiled and said, "You are not the real thing yet.
Why don't you wipe the dirt off your own face?"

30

MAY

A student who felt he had achieved emptiness of mind
boasted to his master, "Now I have no idea."
The master replied, "Why stagger about under the weight
of this concept 'no idea'?"

31

MAY

The truth is to be lived, not just mouthed.

HUI-NENG

1

JUNE

Before he was himself a master, Hakuin went to master Shoju to demonstrate his knowledge of Zen.
When Shoju asked him what he knew, Hakuin pretended to vomit and announced, "Anything I can find I will expel from me." Shoju, however, was unimpressed. He tweaked Hakuin firmly on the nose and said, "What is this? Have I not found something after all?"

2

JUNE

Imitating me won't get you anywhere.
My mind isn't the same as yours. When your mind
is the same as mine, you will be here.

HANSHAN

3

JUNE

"**I** can explain. I know.
I am the teacher you are the student."
Anyone who says such things is guilty
of demonic suggestion.

BAIZHANG

4

JUNE

A monk asked the master, "I've been your student for a long time, but you haven't given me any instruction in the path of Buddhism. Please teach me more."
The master replied, "What do you mean my son?
Every morning you greet me and I greet you back.
You bring me tea which I accept and enjoy drinking.
What more teachings do you want from me?"

5

JUNE

In the situation now before one, and nowhere else,
will Zen be found, or not found at all.

CHRISTMAS HUMPHREYS

6

JUNE

In spring the daffodils bloom
– but not the same daffodils.
And lovers walk in the park
– but not the same lovers.

PETER GANDY

7

JUNE

Twenty monks and one beautiful nun named Eshun were practicing with a master. Several monks fell in love with Eshun and one wrote her a love-letter suggesting a private meeting. Eshun did not reply, but the next day, after the master's talk to the group, she addressed the author saying, "If you love me so much, come and embrace me now."

8

JUNE

There is nothing lukewarm in Zen;
if it is lukewarm, it is not Zen.

D.T. SUZUKI

TAMING 5 THE BULL

The seeker must train his mind to prevent it from forever wandering off into delusion. At this stage the student begins Zen practice in earnest. Such disciplines are not an end in themselves, but a means to harmonize the mind so that it effortlessly expresses the seeker's deeper nature. The bull, once tamed, naturally obeys without struggle or imposed discipline. Kuo-an Shih-yuan writes:

> *With whip and tether*
> *to prevent it wandering off in the wilderness,*
> *the bull will become well trained*
> *and naturally meek —*
> *obeying without need of restraint.*

One thought follows another. When a thought emerges from enlightenment, all thoughts are true — but one deluded thought makes everything false. It is not the objective world that oppresses us, but our own deceiving minds. To master the bull, hold the nose ring tight and do not let your intention vacillate.

9

JUNE

Zen is not a pastime,
but the most serious task in life.

D.T. SUZUKI

10

JUNE

If you don't let go of worldly worries about the future
and making a living, you'll regret it. Follow the Way,
or all your days and nights will have been lived for nothing.

DOGEN

11

JUNE

Is some sickness coming tonight?
Is death waiting for us tomorrow?
There is no greater folly than to be alive
but unconscious — not following the Buddha's Way.

THE VENERABLE CHING

12

JUNE

Zuigan would greet himself each morning and
request of himself, "Today please try and wake up,"
to which he would answer, "Yes, indeed I will."

13

JUNE

Master Seung Sahn taught his students that to let go of
their small self and discover their true self, they must make
a firm decision to attain enlightenment and help others.
To help them they had been given the Buddhist precepts,
but they should know when to keep them and when to
break them, when they are open and when they are closed.

14
JUNE

My compassion to all sentient beings
shall be like the limitless sky.
When released, Mind is freed from
clinging to worldly things.
Even though living in this world of illusion,
My meditations shall be like the lotus flower,
Lovely and unstained, rising up from the mud.
With purified Mind I offer my respects
to the Buddha – The Enlightened One.

ZEN PRAYER AFTER MEALTIMES

15
JUNE

I have no parents; I make heaven and earth my parents.
I have no divine power; I make honesty my power.
I have no means; I make submission my means.
I have no magic power; I make inward strength my magic.
I have neither life nor death; I make Eternity
my life and death.
I have no designs; I make opportunity my design.
I have no miracles; I make the Way my miracle.
I have no principles; I make adaptability
to all things my principle.
I have no friends; I make my mind my friend.
I have no enemy; I make incautiousness my enemy.
I have no armor; I make goodwill and righteousness
my armor.
I have no castle; I make immovable Mind my castle.

SAMURAI'S ZEN CREED

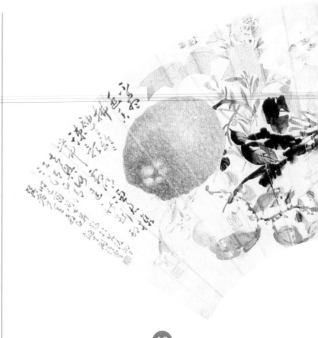

16
JUNE

Tai-an asked master Po-chang, "Help me in my search for the Buddha." Po-chang replied, "It is like looking for an ox when you are riding on one." Tai-an asked, "What should someone who knows this do?" The master answered, "He should ride home on the back of the ox." Tai-an pressed him, "Tell me more." Po-chang said, "Be like a cowherd looking after his cattle, who uses his staff to keep them from wandering off into other pastures."

17
JUNE

Master Kyong Ho taught his students not to hope for a life without problems. Too easy a life leads to a judgmental and lazy mind. He recommended following the ancient proverb: "Accept the anxieties and difficulties of this life."

18
JUNE

Suffering must now be borne, not feared. We caused it, and it will go as soon as we remove its causes and not before.

CHRISTMAS HUMPHREYS

19
JUNE

Acts and thoughts, according to Buddhist doctrines, are creative. What we think and do is never for a moment only, but for measureless time; it signifies some force directed to the shaping of worlds – to the making of future bliss or pain.

LAFCADIO HEARN

20
JUNE

The supreme source of sin lies in greed,
anger, and delusion – the three poisons of the mind.

HUI-NENG

21
JUNE

Buddhism is a ceaseless enemy
to selfish ambition for the aggrandizement of self.

CHRISTMAS HUMPHREYS

22
JUNE

Master Kyong Ho encouraged his students to make
friends but without expecting any benefit for themselves.
Self-centered friendship gets in the way of trust.
He recommended following the ancient proverb:
"Have an enduring friendship with purity of heart."

23
JUNE

Meditation is the reservoir of wisdom,
And the garden of bliss.
Like pure water,
It washes away the dust of desire.
It is armor which protects from evil appetites.
You may not have achieved the state of non-doing,
But you are on your way towards Nirvana.
When agitation rises like dust that obscures the sun,
The rain may damp it down,
The wind of intellectual insight may disperse it,
But only meditation will remove it forever.

CHI-SHA DAISHI

24

JUNE

When you do something,
you should burn yourself completely,
like a good bonfire, leaving no trace of yourself.

SHUNRYU SUZUKI

25

JUNE

The mind is stirred up, all things are stirred up.
The mind is not stirred up, there is nothing stirring.
Nothing has a name.

DAIJU

26

JUNE

If you are consistently not enjoying your meditation
practice, you are doing something wrong.

SHEN T'SING

27

JUNE

Just practicing meditation once
erases countless accumulated sins.

HAKUIN

28

JUNE

If you walk, just walk.
If you sit, just sit.
But don't wobble.

YUNMEN

29

JUNE

A master noticed a student sat all day long in meditation.
"What are you seeking in this way?" he asked.
The pupil replied, "To become a Buddha."
The master picked up a brick and began to polish it on a
stone. "What are you doing?" asked the student.
"Making a mirror," said the master. "You won't make
a mirror by polishing a brick," remarked the student.
"And no amount of sitting cross legged will make
you a Buddha," affirmed the master.

30

JUNE

Whatever we see is changing, losing its balance.
The reason everything looks beautiful is because it is
out of balance, but its background is in perfect harmony.
This is how everything exists in the realm of Buddha nature,
losing its balance against a background of perfect balance.
So if you see things without realizing the background
of Buddha nature, everything appears to be in the form of
suffering. But if you understand the background of
existence, you realize suffering is how we live,
and how we extend our life.

SHUNRYU SUZUKI

1

JULY

Meditation is not Zen.

D.T. SUZUKI

JULY

Hui-ke implored Bodhidharma to be his teacher.
He stood waiting up to his knees in snow while the master
ignored him. It is even said that in despair he cut off his
right arm with a sword to display his earnestness.
Eventually Bodhidharma asked him what he wanted.
Hui-ke asked, "My mind has no peace, please help me
pacify it." Bodhidharma replied, "Bring me your mind
and I will pacify it." Hui-ke was puzzled and eventually said,
"I have searched for my mind, but I cannot find it."
Bodhidharma said, "See! I have already pacified it."

3
JULY

When you know your true self,
the secret is yours.

HUI-NENG

4
JULY

With all your determination, keep asking yourself,
"What is it that hears?" Finally, when you are exhausted with
your questioning, the question will burst and you will feel
reborn from the dead. This is enlightenment.
You will be face to face with all the Buddhas
of all the universes – past and present.

BASSUI TOKUSHO

5
JULY

The Zen Buddhist tradition traces itself to a special
teaching of the Buddha's. One day a large gathering of
followers waited for him to give a sermon on Vulture Peak.
Buddha sat silently for a long time and then lifted a flower
without saying a word. Everyone was dumbfounded,
except old Mahasyapa who smiled. He had experienced the
great awakening, and became the first Buddhist Patriarch.

6
JULY

Give up yourself to others.
Give up yourself to life.
Give up struggling to make sense of it all.
Simply, give up.

T'AO-SHAN

7
JULY

The experience is not the goal of Zen endeavor,
for the will to achieve anything defeats itself;
there is still someone who wants to achieve something,
and there is in truth no seeker, no seeking, and no sought –
all are illusions, veils about the face of Reality.

CHRISTMAS HUMPHREYS

8
JULY

When your mind is always completely empty
you will have achieved purity. But don't think about it or
you'll lose it. If you fall into a state of nonpurity again,
however, simply pay no attention to it
and you will be free once more.

ZEN TEACHING

 9
JULY

Master Chao-chou was sweeping the monastery
when a student asked, "Why do you have to sweep?
You are a great Zen Master free from the dust
of evil thoughts." Chao-chou replied,
"The dust comes from outside."

 10
JULY

Do not be carried away by anything
outward or conventional. Zen must be seized
with bare hands, with no gloves on.

D.T. SUZUKI

 11
JULY

If both sides of the coin can be seen, as it were, at once,
as two sides of a whole, it is easier to be tolerant of the
views expressed by those who see but one of them.

CHRISTMAS HUMPHREYS

JULY

JULY

A monk bowed before a statue of the Buddha and master Chao-chou slapped him. "Is it not praiseworthy to bow before the Buddha?" asked the monk. "Yes," replied the master, "but it is better to do without even a praiseworthy thing."

JULY

Master Huang-po used to bow so much in his Zen practice that he had a a big lump on his forehead. He said, "When I bow, I just bow."

JULY

Burning incense, bowing before the Buddha, offering prayers, confessing your sins, and reading the scriptures – from the very start of one's practice of Zen, these are all completely unnecessary. Liberate yourself from your attachments to body and mind – this is the only requirement. Become the Buddha. If you do, your ecstatic meditations will transform the whole universe into enlightenment.

DOGEN

JULY

There is nothing in this teaching to be argued about. That would be completely against its purpose. Doctrines that encourage debate and controversy cannot free one from birth and death.

HUI-NENG

JULY

It is right in your face. This moment the whole thing is handed to you.

YUAN-WU

JULY

Master Tung-shan was weighing flax when a student asked, "What is Buddha?" Tung-shan replied, "Three pounds of flax."

JULY

Student: *'What is Buddha?'*
Yunmen: *"Dried dung."*

RIDING HOME ON THE BULL

The seeker's once restless and unruly mind is now willingly carrying him toward enlightenment. At this stage the student starts to feel that he is really going somewhere. The world has come to life and he feels a part of its rhythms and harmony. The seeker follows the Way with ease, yet this is far from the end of the journey. Kuo-an Shih-yuan writes:

I ride the bull unhurriedly homeward.
The melody of my song greets the evening.
I beat the pulse, I am the harmony.
There is no need to say
that I am now one of those that know.

The struggle is over. The oxherd is no longer concerned with success or failure. He hums a simple rustic song. Saddled on the bull's back, his attention is not on things of this world. He goes forward, no matter what may attempt to entice him back.

19

JULY

To live – is that not enough? Let us then live, let us affirm!
Herein lie Zen in all its purity and in all its nudity as well.

D.T. SUZUKI

 20

JULY

This world is the Kingdom of Buddha.
This is where enlightenment may be found.
To look for enlightenment by separating from this world
is as crazy as searching for a rabbit's horn!

HUI-NENG

 21

JULY

A truly spiritual person does nothing but continue
with the life he is already living, in the conditions in which
he finds himself. He does not desire to be a Buddha. It never
even crosses his mind.

LIN-CHI

 22

JULY

Don't hang about where you find the Buddha is,
and quickly move on from where he is not to be found.

ZEN SAYING

 23

JULY

Life, according to Zen, should be lived as a bird flies
through the air or as a fish swims in the water.
As soon as there are signs of elaboration, a man is doomed,
he is no more a free being.

D.T. SUZUKI

24
JULY

kkyu's Zen is raw, direct, and authentic.
He was as at home in a brothel as in a temple and talks
with enthusiasm about the joys of sexuality.
Hugging and kissing a young pleasure girl, he reports,
never made him feel like he was burning in hell.
He viewed a puritan saint as nowhere near a Buddha,
and believed Zen was about becoming a natural
human being who enjoyed life to the full.

25
JULY

Having lived the life of a tramp for most of his days, Ikkyu
became the abbot of the most important Zen temple in
Japan. Not long before his death he told his followers that
after he had left them some would become meditative her-
mits in the forests and mountains, while others would drink
wine and frequent brothels. To Ikkyu both of those were
legitimate ways to practice Zen. His only request was that
none of them became professional priests talking nonsense
about the "Way of Zen." Those who chose this path would
not be his students, but his enemies.

26
JULY

Where does my life go?
I sit alone meditating quietly in my hut.
From all my thinking I know nothing.
This is my now. Eternal change and emptiness.
For a while the ego rests here with its "yes and no."
I follow my karma – perfectly content.

RYOKAN

27

JULY

There is no such thing as a time for Zen;
there are twenty-four hours out of every twenty-four.
Zen is a way of living life; more accurately,
living life as life lives itself.

CHRISTMAS HUMPHREYS

28

JULY

Don't meditate so that one day you will become enlightened. Meditate to make your life richer right now.
Meditate when you sit and walk, when you embrace your
mother or care for your child.
Meditate to bring joy into your existence.

SHAN T'SING

29

JULY

Discover who is listening. Find out now!
The dilemmas of birth-and-death are huge and time is
passing. Make the most of it. It won't wait for you.

BASSUI TOKUSHO

30

JULY

Outwardly in the world of good and evil,
yet without thoughts stirring the heart —
this is meditation.
Inwardly seeing one's own true nature
and not being distracted from it —
this is meditation.

HUI-NENG

1

AUGUST

Meditation in movement is a hundred, a thousand,
a million times superior to meditation at rest.

ZEN SAYING

2

AUGUST

Try not to focus your mind anywhere particular,
but rather let it fill all of your body. Let it flow through
your whole being. Then you will find you spontaneously
use your hands when necessary and your legs or eyes when
needed, without wasting time and energy.

**MASTER TAKUAN'S INSTRUCTION
TO THE GREAT SAMURAI YAGYU TAJIMA**

31

JULY

A student of Zen
Walks in Zen and sits in Zen.
Talking and acting,
Or silent and still,
He is always at peace.
He smiles in the face of the executioner.
He remains equanimous,
Even at the moment of death.

YOKA DAISHI

3

AUGUST

It is very important to develop a state of mind called
"immovable wisdom." This doesn't mean be rigid, heavy,
and dead like a rock or block of wood.
On the contrary, it means having complete fluidity
around an unmoving center, so that your mind is clear and
ready to direct its attention wherever it may be needed.

TAKUAN

AUGUST

Zen is a wafting cloud in the sky. No screw fastens it, no string holds it; it moves as it lists. No amount of meditation will keep Zen in one place.

D.T. SUZUKI

AUGUST

Think of moving things as stationary and still things as in motion, then movement and rest will both disappear.

SENG-T'SAN

AUGUST

To simply stop hanging on to what has been in the past and longing for what might be in the future is better than making a ten-year pilgrimage.

LIN-CHI

AUGUST

True meditation is making everything — coughing, swallowing, waving, movement and stillness, speaking and acting, good and evil, fame and shame, loss and gain, right and wrong — into one single koan.

HAKUIN

8

AUGUST

The immovable center within spontaneously responds to whatever presents itself. The mirror of wisdom reflects things the moment they appear, yet is always undisturbed and complete.

TAKUAN

9

AUGUST

You don't need to avoid or deny anything. It is enough to just know about it. When you are busy trying to avoid something, it's still affecting you. Simply cease to be affected or impelled by anything and you'll find you are free.

CAOSHAN

10

AUGUST

Hakuin was admired for living a pure life until one day a young village girl became pregnant and claimed that he was the father. The villagers were angry. When the child was born they presented Hakuin with the baby and told him he must look after it because it was his. Hakuin replied, "Is that so?" and took in the child and cared for it. A year later the girl confessed that the real father was a village boy, and the ashamed villagers went to Hakuin and asked for the child back, saying he was not the father. Hakuin said, "Is that so?" and gave up the baby.

11

AUGUST

When someone doesn't accept what you say, don't attempt to make him understand you intellectually. Don't enter into a debate. Listen to his objections until he begins to find his error himself.

DOGEN

AUGUST

A master and a student were returning to their monastery
when they came across a young woman too fearful to cross
a river. The monks had taken a vow not to look at a woman,
so the young monk turned away. His old master, however,
picked the girl up and carried her across on his shoulders.
Later as they were silently walking the young monk could
contain himself no more and exclaimed, "Why did you pick
up that girl when it is against our vows?" "What?" said the
master. "Are you still carrying that young woman? I put her
down on the other bank of the river."

13
AUGUST

Wisdom is not worth acquiring unless each moment it is applied in acts of Compassion, nor Compassion helpful unless directed by the Wisdom which knows what to do.

CHRISTMAS HUMPHREYS

14
AUGUST

Know the One.
Love the All.

T'AO-SHAN

15
AUGUST

The Buddhist Sutras were available only in Chinese, and Tetsugen wanted to publish them in Japanese. After ten years he had enough donations to complete his project, but at this time there were floods and famine, so he spent the money on relieving suffering. By the time he had collected enough money again, an epidemic engulfed the country and he again spent the money. After twenty years, on his third attempt, he finally published the Sutras in Japanese. The Japanese say he published three sets of Sutras, and that the first two invisible ones were even greater than the last.

16
AUGUST

Think about a piece of music – some great symphony – we don't expect it to get better as it develops, or that its whole purpose is to reach the final crescendo. The joy is found in listening to the music in each moment.

ALAN WATTS

17
AUGUST

Master Seung Sahn encouraged his students just to do what they were doing. He would say, "When eating, just eat. When reading the paper, just read the paper."
A student once discovered Seung Sahn eating while reading the paper. Seung Sahn said, "When eating and reading the paper, just eat and read the paper."

18
AUGUST

Certain actions have been thought of as wrong by past generations, but we do not see anything bad about them now. It may be centuries before there's any clarity about ways we should behave. It's crazy to want immediate approval.

ZENGETSU

A Zen master was invited to the funeral of an illustrious citizen. Half way through the service he walked out. A worried attendant followed him and inquired what was wrong. "This dead man was obviously a hypocrite," said the master, "everyone praises him, and not one person has a bad word to say."

The emperor asked Gudo, "What happens to an enlightened man after death?" Gudo replied, "How should I know, I haven't died yet."

Like Life itself, the enlightened master is both midwife and executioner. Under his impact, the student is reborn, yet paradoxically this is only possible through the death of self. However, paradoxically again, this self has never existed and has always been an illusion. It is perhaps better to talk of being "unborn."

SHEN T'SING

22

AUGUST

Life is fact and no explanation is necessary or pertinent.

D.T. SUZUKI

23

AUGUST

The sudden realization that the Buddha is your own Mind and that there is nothing needing to be achieved nor any idea that must be thought – this is the Great Way.

HUANG-PO

24

AUGUST

One deluded thought and we are dull and ordinary. But with the next awakened thought, we are as wise as the Buddha.

HUI-NENG

25

AUGUST

Every day is a good day.

ZEN SAYING

26

AUGUST

This life is a flash which comes and goes like spring blossoms which fade and fall. Friends, don't fear prospering then passing, like the dew on the morning grass.

VAN-HANH

27

AUGUST

There are many people in this world quietly trying to fulfill the Way, our unknown companions on the path. Everywhere are Bodhisattvas who will be our friends and guide us through the storm of troubles.

THICH THIEN-AN

NO 7 BULL

The seeker arrives home and the bull miraculously disappears. He realizes that the bull has only been a temporary subject of his quest. His search has led to the realization that the separate self, that he previously took himself to be, is not his true nature. The seeker knows his Buddha-nature – his deeper identity. He no longer needs to police himself with whip and tether in hand. He is blissfully at peace. Kuo-an Shih-yuan writes:

Arriving home,
the bull suddenly disappears.
I sit alone at peace.
In blissful release I greet the dawn sun,
with whip and tether abandoned
in my humble homestead.

All is one, not two. The bull is symbolic. You do not need the snare and net, but the hare and fish. Like gold separated from dross or the moon rising from behind the clouds, the One Light shines from the beginning of time.

28

AUGUST

Liang-sui was studying Zen with master Ma-ku who called out his name three times. Each time Liang-sui answered "yes," whereupon the master announced, "You are such a stupid fellow." This brought Liang-sui to his senses and he understood Zen.

29

AUGUST

To study Buddhism is to study your own self.
To study your own self is to forget yourself.

HASHIDA

30

AUGUST

Man suffers because of his craving to possess and keep forever things which are essentially impermanent. Chief among these things is his own person, for this is his means of isolating himself from the rest of life, his castle into which he can retreat and from which he believes he can assert himself against external forces.

ALAN WATTS

31

AUGUST

What we call "I" is just a swinging door which moves when we inhale and when we exhale.

SHUNRYU SUZUKI

1

SEPTEMBER

"What is it that walks toward me?" Hui-neng asked his student Nan-yueh. The student contemplated this question for eight years, then one day it dawned on him and he exclaimed, "Even to say it is a something is to miss the point."

SEPTEMBER

Student: *"What is Zen?"*
Master: *"It is right before your eyes."*
Student: *"So why can't I see it?"*
Master: *"Because you have a Me."*
Student: *"If I know longer have the concept 'Me,'*
will I realize Zen?"
Master: *"If there is no 'Me' who wants to realize Zen?"*

SEPTEMBER

Let go of the idea, "I exist."

IKKYU

SEPTEMBER

This earthly birth
has been crushing me,
but it can't touch me now.

TUE TRUNG

SEPTEMBER

Many deaths follow many births,
in a continual cycle.
Realizing the meaning of "unborn,"
leads beyond joy and grief.

YOKA DAISHI

SEPTEMBER

Wherever I go,
there he is.
He is no other than my self,
but I am not him.

DOSAN

7

S E P T E M B E R

This only is the true Self,
the babe that shall grow and become the universe.

CHRISTMAS HUMPHREYS

8

S E P T E M B E R

Life is an art, and like perfect art
it should be self-forgetting; there ought not
to be any trace of effort or painful feeling.

D.T. SUZUKI

9

S E P T E M B E R

Medicine cures sickness.
All the world is medicine.
What is the self?

YUNMEN

10

S E P T E M B E R

All my sins and failings will disappear when I do.

IKKYU

11

S E P T E M B E R

When you realize Zen, you will see yourself in all beings.
The destitute oppressed and the cruel tyrant that oppresses
them; a hungry child and a bloated landowner; a famous
saint and a notorious rogue; a friend you meet in the market
place and a person you pass while walking whose name you
will never know. All share the one Buddha-nature.

SHEN T'SING

13

SEPTEMBER

Zen teaches us to do good, even when we are alone.

THICH THIEN-AN

14

SEPTEMBER

Push on with all your determination, and just when you feel defeated and blocked, throw yourself into the gaping abyss before you – into the ever-burning flame of your true nature. All illusionary thoughts, feelings, and perceptions will die with your Me, and your Self-nature will appear. You will feel resurrected, truly healthy, and filled with joy and peace.

BASSUI TOKUSHO

12

SEPTEMBER

Ryokan's simple mountain hut was burgled one night. The thief found nothing but the master meditating. Ryokan said, "You have come so far, I can not let you leave empty handed. Here take the clothes I am wearing." The thief left very confused. The master mused, "Poor man, I wish I could have given him this exquisite moon."

15

SEPTEMBER

Satori is the sudden flashing into consciousness of a new truth hitherto undreamed of. It is a sort of mental catastrophe taking place all at once, after much piling up of matters intellectual and demonstrative. The piling has reached a limit of stability and the whole edifice has come tumbling down to the ground, when, behold a new heaven is open to full survey.

D.T. SUZUKI

16

SEPTEMBER

Satori is a flash of intuition deep enough and wide enough to break the barriers of thought in the individual mind, and to let the Whole flood into the part, the relative fragment "see," for a moment of no-time, the Absolute.

CHRISTMAS HUMPHREYS

17

SEPTEMBER

If there is anywhere the least uncertainty, the least feeling of "this is too good to be true," then Satori is only partial, for it implies the desire to cling to the experience lest it should be lost, and until that desire is overcome the experience can never be complete.

ALAN WATTS

18

SEPTEMBER

The corpse which scares you is walking around with you now. Underneath this thin coating of skin, we are already white bones. All of us – rich and poor, man and woman, honored and despised – walking white bones. In death there is no difference, so what do these differences matter now? Meditate on this and you will also find something the same in all of us that could not possibly die, because it was never born.

T'AO-SHAN

19

SEPTEMBER

When you become you, Zen becomes Zen.

SHUNRYU SUZUKI

20

SEPTEMBER

You can't grasp it, but you can't lose it.
It winds its own way.
When you are silent, it speaks.
When you speak, it is dumb.
There are no obstacles.
The great gate of love is wide open.

YUNG-CHIA TA-SHIH

21

SEPTEMBER

A sudden clash of thunder, the mind-doors
burst open, and lo, there sits old man Buddha-nature
in all his homeliness.

CHAO-PIEN

SEPTEMBER

If you want to understand Zen, don't be fooled by others.
Inwardly and outwardly, destroy all obstacles immediately.
If you meet the Buddha, kill him. If you meet the Patriarch,
kill him. Don't hesitate. Kill them all. It's the only way.
Don't get caught up in anything. Rise above. Move on.
Be free!

LIN-CHI

23

SEPTEMBER

Imagine someone suspended from a tree, only able to hold onto a branch with his teeth. Someone else arrives and asks him about Buddhism. If he does not answer he is failing the questioner, but if he opens his mouth he will lose his life. What is his way out of this predicament?

HSIANG-YEN

24

SEPTEMBER

It is traditionally said that when the Buddha was born he exclaimed, "Above and below the heavens, I alone am the Honored One." Master Yunmen commented, "If I had been with him when he said this, I would have killed him with a single blow and thrown his corpse to the hungry dogs."

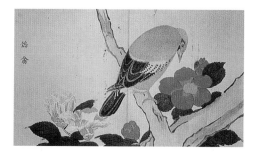

25

SEPTEMBER

Master Nan-ch'uan discovered a group of monks quarreling about the ownership of a cat. To show them the consequences of such craziness, he threatened to cut the cat in two unless someone could say something to save the poor animal. No one said a word, so the master cut the the cat in two. Sometime later Chao-chou returned to the monastery. Nan-ch'uan related what had happened and asked what he would have done to save the animal. Without a moment's hesitation Chao-chou removed his straw sandals, put them on his head and left the room. Nan-ch'uan mused, "If Chao-chou had been here, that cat would still be alive."

26

SEPTEMBER

Enter in. Be one with the object of contemplation if you wish to understand. Don't be an outside observer of life. Be life.

T'AO-SHAN

NO ANYTHING

If all is one, then no separate things exist. All merges into No-thing. The self for which the seeker has been seeking, has no independent reality. It dissolves into the Oneness. This is the experience of Nirvana, the extinguishing of self – the knowledge of emptiness represented in traditional paintings of this stage as an empty circle. There is no longer anything to be achieved, because there is no one to achieve anything. Although the vision that the seeker has been seeking has finally been attained, there is no separate self to glory in this achievement. Kuo-an Shih-yuan writes:

> *Whip and tether, self and bull —*
> *every thing is no thing.*
> *The clear blue sky is unmarked by a message.*
> *Could a snowflake persist in a flaming fire?*
> *This is the place of the ancient masters.*

Mind, clear of all limitations. Confusion is replaced by serenity. Ideas of holiness are irrelevant. He is not enlightened, but he is not unenlightened. When there is no duality, a thousand eyes could not see any division. Even if birds dropped flowers where he walked, all praise would be without meaning.

27

SEPTEMBER

Only by accepting that the ego is a fabricated
illusion do we walk the Buddha's Way.

DOGEN

28

SEPTEMBER

Surrender everything – your body, your life,
your inner self – and you will experience peace,
ease, nondoing, and inexpressible happiness.

YUAN-WU

29

SEPTEMBER

Zen is easy. It is only selfishness
which is problematic and painful.

SHEN T'SING

30

SEPTEMBER

Forgoing self, the universe grows I.

ZEN SAYING

1

OCTOBER

On seeing the peach flowers,
Abbot Rei-Un became enlightened.
As did Master Kyo-Gen,
At hearing the crack of a bamboo.

2

OCTOBER

Any previous doubts dissolved completely like thawing ice.
I exclaimed, "Wonderful! Wonderful! No birth and death to
be liberated from. No ultimate understanding to strive
after."

A MASTER'S DESCRIPTION OF HIS ENLIGHTENMENT

3

OCTOBER

After years of arduous struggle, Ikkyu was meditating in a
boat one midsummer night when he heard the caw of a
crow and was spontaneously enlightened. When his master
Kaso present him with an "inka," a seal of enlightenment,
Ikkyu just threw it to the ground and walked away saying
he needed no official approval. Kaso said, "Undoubtedly
Ikkyu is my heir, but his way is to be wild." Ikkyu continued
to live an eccentric and spontaneous life, calling himself
"Crazy Cloud."

4

OCTOBER

If you are seen as great or wise by others,
you have not yet reached maturity.

GEMPO YAMAMOTO

5

OCTOBER

Once we have freed ourselves from the ego-illusion, we
must awaken our inner wisdom, the pure and divine Buddha
Mind. It is the divine light, the inner heaven, the key to
moral riches, the source of all influence and power, the root
of kindness, justice, sympathy, impartial love, humanity, and
mercy, the measure of all things.

KAITEN NUKARIYA

6

OCTOBER

When the mind is ready for some reasons or others,
a bird flies, or a bell rings, and you at once return to your
original home.

D.T. SUZUKI

7

OCTOBER

Hung-jen, the fifth Zen Patriarch, was seeking a successor. He asked his monks to display their insight by writing a verse. The hot favorite for the post Shen-hsiu wrote:

The body is like the Bodhi tree.

The mind is like a perfect mirror.

Be careful to always keep it clean,

And unobscured by the dust of impurities.

The master was not over impressed. On reading this verse, an illiterate kitchen worker named Hui-neng asked a friend to write down the following and present it to the master.

There is no Bodhi-tree.

There is no mirror.

Everything is void.

What could dust possibly cover?

Hui-neng became the sixth and last Zen Patriarch.

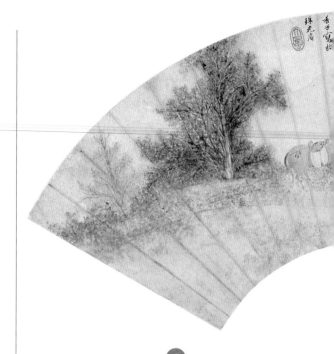

9

OCTOBER

Student: *"What is the mind?"*

Master: *"Mind is the Buddha."*

Student: *"Thank you. Now I see."*

Master: *"Now that you see I say the truth is there is no mind and no Buddha."*

Student: *"Then why did you say 'The mind is the Buddha'?"*

Master: *"I had to stop the baby crying."*

8

OCTOBER

Student: *"Are words the Mind?"*

Daiju: *"No. Words are objective, they are not the Mind."*

Student: *"Ignoring words then, what is Mind?"*

Daiju: *"There is no Mind independent of words."*

Student: *"Then what is the Mind?"*

Daiju: *"Mind is without form or image.*

Actually it is neither independent of nor dependent upon words. It is always free and unmoving."

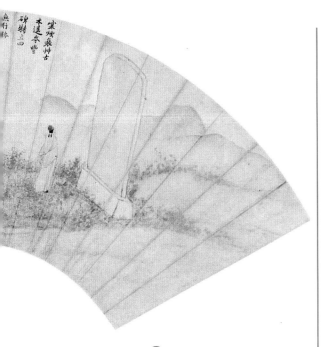

10

OCTOBER

Your original Face cannot be placed anywhere in particular. It will still be, even when the universe ends.

YUNMEN

11

OCTOBER

Tung-shan: *"I show the truth to living beings."*
Student: *"What are they like then?"*
Tung-shan *"No longer living beings."*

12

OCTOBER

Zen can be defined as the unity of man and the universe, as the rhythm of the mind with changing forms, as a state of "One-ness" in which all distinctions of "I" and "not-I," knower and known, seer and seen, are set aside.

ALAN WATTS

13

OCTOBER

Everything is interrelated. Nothing exists alone. Without me speaking these words you could not hear them. Without my parents I would not be, and without their parents they would not be. Without the sun and rain that nurtured the crops and the farmer who cultivated them, and the baker who baked the bread, they would not have had food. Without the earth to support us and the air to breathe, how would we be sustained? Ultimately, what can be said to exist without every other thing? All things are parts of One Thing. This is not a clever idea, it is the Truth.

T'AO-SHAN

OCTOBER

All phenomena the Buddha says are Mu, empty and void. Why does the Buddha say this? Because all phenomena arise and exist through the combination of many different elements. Since what exists depends upon other things for existence, it lacks an immutable core of independent actuality and is, therefore, considered in itself, void.

THICH THIEN-AN

OCTOBER

Master Ekai meditated on "mu" for six years, until one day he heard the monastery drum and was enlightened. He gave the following advice to students meditating on the koan: "Concentrate on 'mu' with your whole self, every bone and pore, until it makes you a solid lump of doubt. Day and night, without stopping, keep digging into it. Don't view it as 'nothingness' or as 'being' or as 'non-being.' Make it a red-hot iron ball which you have swallowed down and want to vomit up – but just can't. Forget all illusionary thoughts and feelings that are dear to you. After some time of making this effort, 'mu' will bear fruit, and, quite spontaneously, inside and out will become one. You will end up like a dumb man who has awoken from dreaming. You will know yourself – but only for yourself. 'Mu' will suddenly explode shaking the earth and opening the heavens."

16

OCTOBER

Mu is a third possibility, beyond "yes and no."
It says that affirming or denying will not answer the
question. Such replies would be too limited for the
Truth of the answer.

SHAN T'SING

17

OCTOBER

A monk asked Chao-chou, "Does a dog have Buddha-
nature?" Chao-chou answered with an exclamation of "wu!"
(Japanese "mu"). D.T. Suzuki remarks that Chao-chou's
answer is no mystery. His "wu" means simply "wu" – it is
what the dog himself would have said.

18

OCTOBER

Master Shou-shan began his sermon by producing
a stick and declaring, "Call this a stick and you assert
something untrue. Call it not a stick and you negate
something obvious. Now, without asserting and negating –
what would you call it? Come on! Speak!" A monk jumped
up and broke the stick in two saying, "What is this?"

19

OCTOBER

The Truth cannot be found.
If you say you see it,
it is not the Truth.
Leave things alone,
and there is nothing false,
just Mind itself.
When Mind is bound by the false
there is no Truth to be found anywhere.

HUI-NENG

OCTOBER

The phenomenal universe is like a film projected onto a blank screen. The film is a continual series of ever-changing pictures. Through our ignorance we may become attached to the figures on the screen. We may laugh with them or cry with them, swell with pride or grow tense with excitement, but this does not make them real, and once the projector stops, all those figures with whom we have been so deeply involved will vanish into nothingness, together with all their loves and hates, their joys and sorrows, their adventures and intrigues. The world is just like a movie on the screen; evanescent, insubstantial, and void. Even this very being we call our "self" dissolves upon analysis into a mere appearance destitute of final actuality.

THICH THIEN-AN

OCTOBER

Two monks were arguing. One said, "The flag is moving." The other said, "No, the wind is moving." On hearing their dispute Hui-neng said, "It is neither the flag nor the wind that is moving. It is your mind that moves."

22

OCTOBER

A nun named Miaoxin overheard a group of monks arguing about whether the flag moved, the wind moved, or the mind moved. All of them admitted they did not understand. Miaoxin said to herself, "What a shame, these poor monks haven't seen the Way of the Buddha even in their dreams." Someone overheard her comments and reported them to the monks. Feeling humbled they asked her for teachings. She told them, "It is not the wind that moves. It is not the flag that moves. It is not the mind that moves."

23

OCTOBER

As a young student of Zen, Yamaoka Tesshu visited Master Dokuon. Hoping to show off his understanding of Buddhist philosophy he said, "In reality nothing exists – not the mind, nor the Buddha, nor any sentient beings. Emptiness is the source of all phenomena. There is no enlightenment and no delusion, no wise man and no average man. There is no giving and nothing is receiving." Dokuon sat silently smoking his bamboo pipe, ignoring the pupil who become increasingly agitated. Suddenly Dokuon whacked Yamaoka hard with his pipe, which made him yell with anger. "If nothing exists," inquired Dokuon, "where did this anger come from?"

24

OCTOBER

There is only the one Way – straight, open, and utterly empty of obstructions.

YUAN-WU

25

OCTOBER

The man made of wood starts to sing. The woman made of stone starts to dance. This cannot happen through learning or logic.

TUNG-SHAN

26

OCTOBER

A 16-year-old girl named Satsu soon became awakened after studying with Hakuin. One day her father found her meditating while sitting on a box. "What are you doing!" he exclaimed. "There is a statue of the Buddha in that box." The young girl replied to her astonished father, "If there is any place where the Buddha does not exist – take me there."

RETURNING TO THE SOURCE

In older Taoist versions of the "Bulls" story, the destination is reached at step eight. But the Zen masters perceived that in such a state there still remained a subtle remnant of duality, for there is still "Nirvana" and its opposite "Samsara" – the void and the world of appearances, the One and the All. A further growth in awareness is necessary, and when the seeker reaches the Source he sees that there is no difference between Nirvana and Samsara. They are two indivisible sides of One Reality. He has always been where he needed to be. Things simply are what they are. Everything is just happening. Kuo-an Shih-yuan writes:

> *I have returned to the root and effort is over.*
> *From the first there has been no one*
> *to see or hear anything.*
> *There is nothing outside of my true home.*
> *Rivers quietly flow and red flowers bloom.*

From the beginning he has been pure, immaculate, and without stain. He witnesses that which is being created and destroyed, from a place of unmoving serenity. He does not identify with the illusion of separateness. The waters are blue and the mountains are green; he calmly watches all things changing.

29

OCTOBER

All Buddhas and all sentient beings are nothing
but expressions of the One Mind. There is nothing else.
This Mind has no beginning. It is unborn and unending.

HUANG-PO

30

OCTOBER

When I say "yes" I don't affirm anything, and when I say
"no" I don't negate anything. I stand above "yes" and "no."
There is just this state of absolute purity – stark and naked.

YUAN-WU

31

OCTOBER

Here is the unsophisticated self, your original face.
Here is the landscape of your birthplace, bare and beautiful.

YUAN-WU

27

OCTOBER

When everything is seen as One, we return to the Source
and stay where we have always been.

SENG-T'SAN

28

OCTOBER

We have all, need nothing, are everything.
And all is one, just one, not two.

CHRISTMAS HUMPHREYS

1

NOVEMBER

All things are empty.

They have no beginning and no end.

They are faultless and not faultless.

They are not perfect and not imperfect.

In this emptiness there is no form,

No perception, no names, no concepts, no knowledge.

There is no decay, nor death.

There are no Four Noble Truths —

No suffering, no origin of suffering,

no cessation of suffering,

And no path to the cessation of suffering.

There is no knowledge of Nirvana,

No obtaining it and no not obtaining it.

ZEN RECITATION BEFORE MEALTIMES

2

NOVEMBER

Understand that Mind is no Mind, and you will understand
Mind and its workings.

BODHIDHARMA

3

NOVEMBER

Years of digging the earth searching for the blue sky,
piling up layer upon layer of mediocrity.
Then one dark night the ceiling blew off,
and the whole structure disappeared into emptiness.

MUSO

4

NOVEMBER

The light of Consciousness embraces the whole universe.

PAN-SHAN

5

NOVEMBER

It is like seeing light in deep darkness or receiving
riches in poverty. You become open and clear. You see into
the essential nature of things, which now seem like flowers
in a fairy tale without any tangible reality.

YUAN-WU

6

NOVEMBER

The silence is not that of the desert shorn of all vegetation,
nor is it that of a corpse forever gone to sleep and decay.
It is the silence of an "eternal abyss" in which all contrasts
and conditions are buried; it is the silence of God who,
deeply absorbed in contemplation of his works past,
present, and future, sits calmly on his throne of absolute
oneness and allness.

D.T. SUZUKI

A conquering tyrant and his armies were sweeping through the country, laying waste all before them. When they arrived at a certain village, all the inhabitants had taken refuge in the surrounding hills, except for one old monk. The tyrant was enraged at the impudence of the monk and personally stormed into the monastery and confronted him face to face. "Don't you know who I am?" he bellowed at the still, quiet master. "I could draw my sword and cut you in two and not blink an eye." The master smiled serenely and replied, "Don't you know who I am? I could stand here while you draw your sword and cut me in two, and not blink an eye."

7
NOVEMBER

The big mind in which we must have confidence is not something you can experience objectively. It is something which is always with you, always on your side. Your eyes are on your side, for you cannot see your eyes, and your eyes cannot see themselves. Eyes only see things outside, objective things. If you reflect on your self, that self is not your true self any more. You cannot project yourself as an objective thing to think about. The mind which is always on your side is not just your mind, it is universal mind, always the same, not different to another's mind. It is Zen mind. It is big, big mind.

SHUNRYU SUZUKI

9
NOVEMBER

Te-shan used to carry copies of the scriptures with him wherever he went, until the day of his enlightenment when he set fire to them, reducing them all to ashes, exclaiming, "No matter how profound one's understanding of philosophy, it is like a hair floating in vast space. No matter how wide one's worldly experience, it is like a drop of water falling into an unfathomable abyss."

NOVEMBER

Your mind free, silent and sufficient.
It exists above all forms

YUAN-WU

NOVEMBER

Tao-wu asked master Shih-t'ou, "What is the essence of Buddhism?" The master replied, "Not to achieve, not to know." Tao-wu asked, "Is there a turning point in going beyond or not?" The master said, "The empty sky does not hinder the passing clouds."

NOVEMBER

From the first not a thing is.

HUI-NENG

NOVEMBER

All my worries and problems have left me.
I am happily playing far away from the world.
There are no limits for someone with Zen.
The blue sky must feel ashamed to be so small.

MUSI SOSEKI

NOVEMBER

Sixty-six times,
I've seen this change to autumn.
Enough talk about moonlight.
Don't ask for more.
Just listen now
To the tree voices
When no breeze blows.

RYO-NEN

15

NOVEMBER

Speech is blasphemy, Silence is deception.
Beyond both is a way up, but my mouth
is not wide enough to point to it.

I - T U A N

16

NOVEMBER

The reality of Mind is without any distinct form.
It permeates everything. In the eye it becomes seeing.
In the ear it becomes hearing. In the nose it becomes
smelling. In the mouth it becomes talking. In the hand
it becomes touching. In the feet it becomes walking.
Everything is originally one spiritual light which
harmoniously diversifies. Mind has no definite form
and so acts in every form.

L I N - C H I

17

NOVEMBER

A cluster of summer trees.
A glimpse of the sea.
A pale evening moon.

K O B O R I   E N S H I U

18

NOVEMBER

It is totally indescribable and completely inexpressible,
for there is nothing worldly to compare it to. The world of
myriad sense-objects now seemed transformed. What I
hated before, including my passions and ignorance, now
appeared as no more than the outpouring of my innermost
nature, which always remained light, true, and clear.

A   M A S T E R ' S   D E S C R I P T I O N   O F   H I S   E N L I G H T E N M E N T

NOVEMBER

The Way is not about knowing or not-knowing.
Knowing is only delusion and
not-knowing is merely blank consciousness.

NAN-CH'UAN

20

NOVEMBER

There is good and there is bad
– and that is good.
There is perfection and there is imperfection
– and that is perfect.

T'AO-SHAN

21

NOVEMBER

When the Buddha achieved enlightenment
under the Bodhi tree, he laughed.

THICH THIEN-AN

22

NOVEMBER

Master Pai-chang was approached by a fox who told him,
"I once was a Zen master and one of my students asked me
if an enlightened man was subject to the law of causation.
I replied, 'The enlightened man rides the wave of causation.'
For this error I was condemned to live as a fox for five hundred lives. Please help me see my mistake."
Pai-chang told him, "For the enlightened man, there is only
the wave of causation." His visitor became enlightened
and the fox was no more.

23

NOVEMBER

Understand the Abrupt Doctrine
and external disciplines are unnecessary.

HUI-NENG

24

NOVEMBER

The teachings expounded in the Taoist,
Confucian, and Buddhist scriptures are merely
commentaries on the spontaneous cry – "Ah, this!"

DAIE

25

NOVEMBER

When the curious ask you what It is,
Don't affirm or deny anything.
Anything affirmed is not true,
Anything denied is not true.
How can someone say what It is
When he has not fully known It?
And, knowing, what letters can be sent
From a land where words find no road to travel?
To their questions, therefore, offer silence.
Only silence and a pointing finger.

ZEN POEM

RETURNING TO THE WORLD

The final step is back into the world. The student, now a master, lives an ordinary life among ordinary folk, yet in him all opposites are reconciled. He exists, but not as a "something" separate from the rest of Life. He is simply at One with everything. He is a completely natural human being. He perceives that everything is perfect just as it is. Whether they know it or not, he sees that everyone is already enlightened, just as he himself has been all along. He has not become a master with special magical powers, but a simple witness of the spontaneous unfolding of the supreme miracle that is life itself. Kuo-an Shih-yuan writes:

> *Barefoot and plain, I mingle in the market place.*
> *My clothes may be ragged, but I am smiling.*
> *I need no magical powers.*
> *Before my eyes the withered trees bloom.*

A thousand sages don't know who he is. The beauty of his garden cannot be seen. Why search for the footprints of the Patriarch? He visits the market place with his empty wine bottle and walks back home with his staff. He keeps the company of drunkards and butchers and everyone he sees is enlightened.

26

NOVEMBER

Empress Wu became fascinated with the relationship between the essential Oneness and the apparent multiplicity of life. She asked Fa-tsang if he could give a simple, practical demonstration to help her understand. Fa-tsang arranged one of the palace rooms so that eight large mirrors stood at the eight points of the compass. He then placed a further mirror on the floor, and another on the ceiling. A candle was suspended in the center of the room, and the Empress was invited in. Fa-tsang then lit the candle and the room was filled with the splendor of reflected light. The Empress Wu was awed and overcome by the beauty of this vision. "You see, your majesty," said the master. "This is the One and the many."

27

NOVEMBER

Enlightenment is like the reflection of the moon in water. The moon does not get wet and the water is not separated.

HASHIDA

28

NOVEMBER

The Supreme Wisdom is the Oneness of things;
The Supreme Compassion is the Manyness of things.

D.T. SUZUKI

29

NOVEMBER

Clinging to the void and neglecting compassion does not lead to the highest realization. Practicing only compassion does not bring release from the toils of existence.
He, however, who is strong in both, remains neither in Samsara nor in Nirvana.

ZEN TEACHING

2

DECEMBER

Understanding and loving are indivisible.
Great understanding comes with great love.

T'AO-SHAN

3

DECEMBER

As long as you remain in one extreme
or another you will never know Oneness.

SENG-T'SAN

30

NOVEMBER

Wisdom and Compassion are inseparable.

CHRISTMAS HUMPHREYS

1

DECEMBER

The universe is totally permeated by love-play
from animal lust to sublime compassion,
and every shade in between.

ALAN WATTS

4

DECEMBER

One perfect Nature pervades and circulates
within all natures.
One all-inclusive Reality contains and
embraces all realities.
One moon is reflected in every expanse of water.
Every reflected moon is the one moon.

YUNG-CHIA TA-SHIH

5

DECEMBER

Hui-neng taught that nondoing is a reality,
the truth is emptiness, and the meaning of things is found in
the vast and immovable. He viewed human nature,
from its beginning to its end, as completely good and not in
need of any unnatural weeding, for it is rooted in serenity.

INSCRIPTION ON HUI-NENG'S TOMBSTONE

6

DECEMBER

When master Tung-shan was dying his successor
Ts'ao-shun asked him, "Where are you going?"
The master replied, "I go where it is changeless."
His student asked, "How can you go where it is changeless?"
The master replied, "My going is no change."

7

DECEMBER

I won't die.
I won't go anywhere.
Just don't ask me anything.

IKKYU

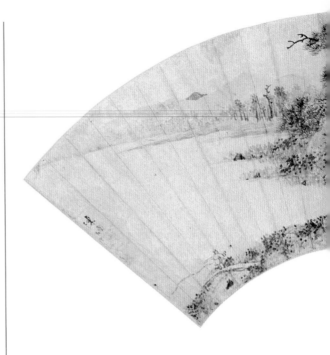

8

DECEMBER

It is traditional for Zen masters to write a final verse
before their deaths. One master was almost passing away
and had not performed this requirement which his students
urged him to undertake. Eventually before letting out his
last breath he reluctantly took a pen and scrawled –

Life is thus,
Death is thus,
Verse or no verse,
What's the fuss?

10

DECEMBER

Moment after moment, everything
comes out of nothingness.
This is the true joy of life.

SHUNRYU SUZUKI

11

DECEMBER

On his deathbed the modern Zen master
Shunryu Suzuki was asked by a student where they would
meet in the future. He silently drew a circle in the air.

9

DECEMBER

Spring blossom.
Cuckoos in the hills.
Autumn leaves.
These will be my legacy.

RYOKAN

12

DECEMBER

One glimpse of the true human being,
And we are in love.

IKKYU

13

DECEMBER

When Master Daito met Emperor Godaiga, who was a student of Zen, he said, "Thousands of ages ago we were separated, yet not for a moment have we been apart. We have never met, yet we face each other all day long."

14

DECEMBER

Even to hold to Oneness is to miss it.

TAO-WU

15

DECEMBER

With all our philosophy, with all our grand and enhancing ideas, we cannot escape life as we live it. Star-gazers are still walking on the solid earth.

D.T. SUZUKI

16

DECEMBER

One embraces All
All merges in One
One is All.
All is One.
One pervades All.
All is in One.

TEACHING OF KEGON SCHOOL

17

DECEMBER

The One and the All. Mingle and move
without discriminating. Live in this awareness
and you'll stop worrying about not being perfect.

SENG-T'SAN

18

DECEMBER

Now. This is it.
The whole purpose and meaning for the existence
of everything.

ALAN WATTS

 19

DECEMBER

How wonderful!
Quite miraculous!
I am fetching water
And carrying wood!

P'ANG·YUN

20

DECEMBER

Zen opens a man's eye to the greatest mystery
as it is daily and hourly performed; it enlarges the heart to
embrace eternity of time and infinity of space in its every
palpitation; it makes us live in the world as if walking
in the garden of Eden.

D.T. SUZUKI

21

DECEMBER

The limitless sky of meditation.
The clear moonlight of wisdom.
The truth revealed as eternal stillness.
This earth is the pure lotus-land.
This body is the body of the Buddha.

HAKUIN

22

DECEMBER

It is a kind of a mystery that for people
who have no experiences of enlightenment, enlightenment
is something wonderful. But if they attain it, it is nothing.
But yet it is not nothing. Do you understand? For a mother
with children, having children is nothing special.

SHUNRYU SUZUKI

23

DECEMBER

Silently sitting by the window.
Leaves fall and flowers bloom.
The seasons come and go.
Could there be a better life?

ZEN POEM

24

DECEMBER

From the beginning nothing has been kept from you,
all that you wished to see has been there all the time before
you, it was only yourself that closed the eye to the fact.

D.T. SUZUKI

25

DECEMBER

The mind becomes the Buddha without altering
its nature from that with which it came into being at birth.
So what is there to pray for?

SHEN T'SING

26

DECEMBER

Student: *"What is the Buddha?"*
Ma'tsu: *"This Mind is the Buddha."*

27

DECEMBER

Language!
The Way is not words.
It knows no past,
No future,
No now.

SENG-T'SAN

28

DECEMBER

Any book about Zen is rather like
a mystery story with the last chapter missing.

ALAN WATTS

29

DECEMBER

Student: *"What is the Buddha?"*
Ma'tsu: *"No-Mind is the Buddha."*

30

DECEMBER

Not this, not that, not anything.

ZEN TEACHING

31

DECEMBER

To the man without understanding,
the world is as it is.
To the man with understanding,
the world is as it is.

HSUAN-SHA

GLOSSARY

Zen terms that may be unfamiliar to some readers

Bodhisattva — An awakened master who renounces merging with Nirvana so as to serve others on the path to enlightenment.

Bodhi tree — Bodhi means "knowledge" or "enlightenment." The Bodhi tree is the tree under which the Buddha sat in meditation until he received his enlightenment.

Buddha — The name for an enlightened being, usually used to refer to Sakyamuni Buddha, the fifth century B.C. Indian founder of Buddhism.

Buddha-nature — The self experienced without separateness from all that is.

Dharma — The way the universe works. The law on which the processes of life are based. The teachings of the Buddha. The nature of things in general, or if applied to something in particular, the law that governs its essential being.

Karma — The law of cause and effect, according to which one's past actions create one's future destiny.

Koan — A word or phase used as a subject for meditation that cannot be understood by the rational mind, but may help the practitioner break through into a deeper state of consciousness.

Nirvana — Total release from karma. The extinguishing of the self and the complete realization of the emptiness of all forms of separateness.

Patriarch — A term meaning "father" applied to the founders and early influential contributors to Buddhism.

Samsara — The world of appearances and ever-changing flux. The illusion of separateness. The wheel of reincarnation that leads a soul through many births in its search of enlightenment.

Sanskrit — The sacred language of ancient India.

Satori — An experience of a state of consciousness beyond duality and differentiation in which all is One. This may be a transitory glimpse of a final enlightenment that will take years to mature.

Sutras and Sastras — Buddhist scriptures.

Taoism — Chinese religion that pre-exists oriental Buddhism and greatly influenced Zen. The Tao is the "Way," comparable in many respects to the Buddhist word "Dharma."

Zazen — Zen meditation.